Our Field Trip

Gathering Data

Mitchell Allen

COMPUTER SCIENCE For the REAL World™

My class plans a trip.

Miss Todd takes a vote.

8 kids vote for the zoo.

5 kids vote for the park.

9 kids vote for the farm.

We go to the farm!

Words to Know

farm

park

zoo